**WAY**

j551
Cole, Joanna.
The magic school bus at the
    waterworks

P9-EDY-310

DO NOT REMOVE
CARDS FROM POCKET

WAYNEDALE BRANCH LIBRARY
2200 LOWER HUNTINGTON RD.
FORT WAYNE, IN 46819

ALLEN COUNTY PUBLIC LIBRARY

FORT WAYNE, INDIANA 46802

You may return this book to any agency, branch,
or bookmobile of the Allen County Public Library.

# The Magic School Bus
## At the Waterworks

# The Magic School Bus
# At the Waterworks

*By Joanna Cole*   *Illustrated by Bruce Degen*

SCHOLASTIC INC. / *New York*

SCHOLASTIC
HARDCOVER

Allen County Public Library
Ft. Wayne, Indiana

*The author and illustrator wish to thank Nancy Zeilig and
the technical services staff at American Water Works Association,
Denver, Colorado, for their help in preparing this book.*

Text copyright © 1986 by Joanna Cole.
Illustrations copyright © 1986 by Bruce Degen.
All rights reserved. Published by Scholastic Inc. SCHOLASTIC HARDCOVER is a trademark of Scholastic Inc.
Art direction/design by Diana Hrisinko.

No part of this publication may be reproduced in whole or in part,
or stored in a retrieval system, or transmitted in any form or by any means,
electronic, mechanical, photocopying, recording, or otherwise,
without written permission of the publisher.
For information regarding permission, write to Scholastic Inc.,
730 Broadway, New York, NY 10003.

Library of Congress Cataloging-in-Publication Data
Cole, Joanna.
The magic school bus.
Summary: When Ms. Frizzle, the strangest teacher
in school, takes her class on a field trip to the
waterworks, everyone ends up experiencing the water
purification system from the inside.
[1.Water treatment plants—Fiction.   2. School
excursions—Fiction.   3. Teachers—Fiction]   I. Degen,
Bruce, ill.   II. Title.
PZ7.C67346Mag   1986     [E]       86-6672
ISBN 0-590-40361-3

12  11  10   9   8   7   6   5   4   3   2   1      10      6   7   8  9/8   0   1/9

Printed in the U.S.A.                                                10

W 2288672

To Rachel

J.C.

For Uncle Jerry,
the Water Chemist

B.D.

Our class really has bad luck.
This year, we got Ms. Frizzle,
the strangest teacher in school.

We don't mind Ms. Frizzle's strange dresses.
Or her strange shoes.
It's the way she acts that really gets us.
Ms. Frizzle makes us grow green mold
on old pieces of bread.
She makes us build clay models of garbage dumps,
draw diagrams of plants and animals,
and read five science books a week.

HOW MOLD GROWS
by Amanda Jane and Arnold

LISTEN, ARNOLD. IT'S LEARNING TO TALK!

GURGLE MMFF

DOES THAT MEAN WE'LL GET AN "A"?

Other classes go on trips to the zoo,
or even the circus.
Guess where we went on our class trip.
To the waterworks!

And to get ready for the trip,
Ms. Frizzle made us
spend a whole month in the library.
We had to find out exactly
how our city gets its water —
down to the last drop.
We also had to collect
ten interesting facts about water.

In the parking lot,
the old school bus was waiting.
To our surprise,
there was no bus driver.
Instead, The Friz herself
was behind the wheel.

At the end of the block
the bus went into a dark tunnel.
When we came out, something amazing
had happened.
The bus looked a lot different.
We looked different, too.
Everyone was wearing
a scuba diving outfit!
Even Ms. Frizzle.

WATER FACT #3
by Shirley
There is water in the air you are breathing. You can't see it, because it is in the form of an invisible gas called water vapor.
When water <u>evaporates</u>, it changes from a liquid to a gas and rises into the air.

I DIDN'T KNOW THAT!

WE'RE GOING UP!

Ms. Frizzle was the only one who didn't seem to notice the change. She just drove on. In the middle of a bridge, the bus started...

to rise into...

14

Then Ms. Frizzle did
the weirdest thing ever.
She told everybody to get
out of the bus!
The kids didn't want to go.
But Frizzie threatened to give
extra homework if we didn't.

I'LL TAKE THE
HOMEWORK.

Some kids stuck their heads
out of the cloud and looked down.
There were mountains down there!
And the cloud was going higher
every minute.

It was getting colder, too.
All around us,
drops of water began to form.
And as the drops got bigger,
we got smaller!

Before long, each kid was
the size of a raindrop.
In fact, each kid was
*in* a raindrop.
The drops began to fall.
Ms. Frizzle's class was raining!

We fell into a clear mountain stream
and began flowing
down the mountainside.

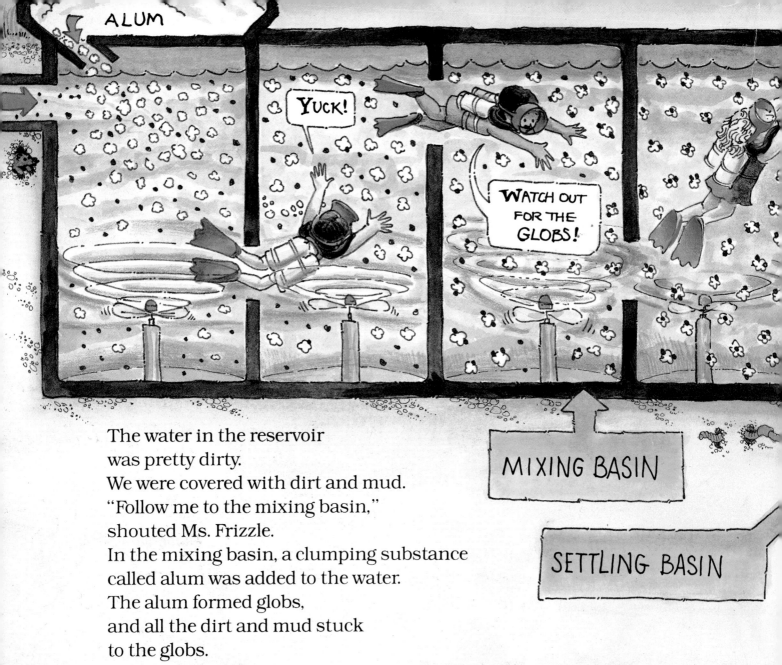

The water in the reservoir
was pretty dirty.
We were covered with dirt and mud.
"Follow me to the mixing basin,"
shouted Ms. Frizzle.
In the mixing basin, a clumping substance
called alum was added to the water.
The alum formed globs,
and all the dirt and mud stuck
to the globs.

"On to the settling basin!"
ordered The Friz.
There the globs sank to the bottom,
and the clean water flowed off the top.
Now we were on our way to the filter.

This was the sand-and-gravel filter
that takes out any impurities
still in the water.
We were impurities,
we couldn't get through!
Luckily, Ms. Frizzle showed us
a special way around the filter.
When the water came out of the filter,
it was sparkling clear.

WATER FACT #7
by MOLLY

Clear water is not
always clean water.
It may still contain
disease germs
that can make
you sick.

In the pipe from the filter
to a storage tank, a chemical called
chlorine was added to the water.
Chlorine kills any remaining disease germs.
A trace of fluoride was also added
to keep kids from getting
so many cavities.

The water had come all the way
through the purification system.
We thought our class trip was over.
But Frizzie had other ideas.
"Everybody into the storage
tank," she shouted.

FLUORIDE

CHLORINE

WATER FACT #8
by Amanda Jane
The first pipes in North America were made of hollowed-out logs. Today pipes are made of concrete, metal, even plastic.

Before we knew what was happening, we were whooshed out of the tank and into a pipe that carries water to our city.

WHERE'S THE BUS?

FOLLOW ME, CLASS.

Then we went into water mains, the pipes that run under the city streets.

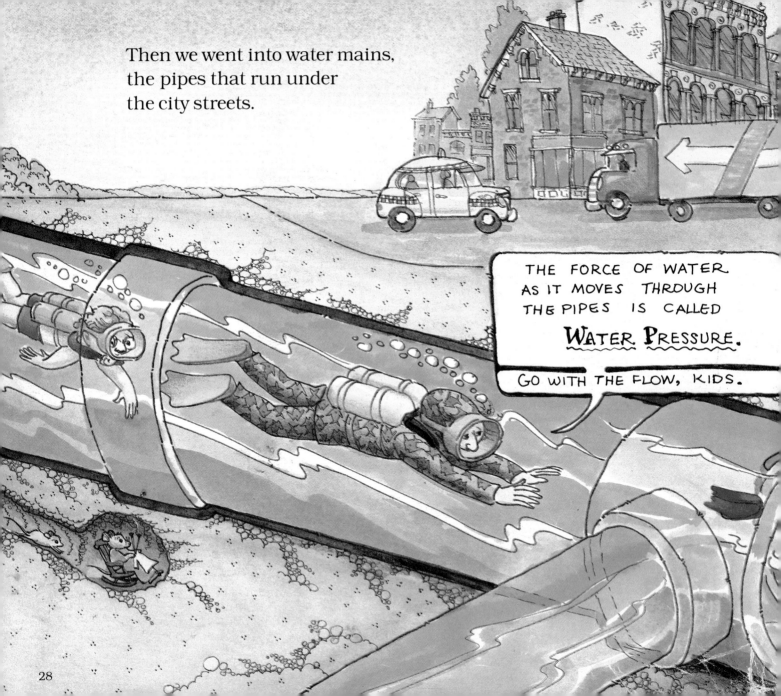

THE FORCE OF WATER AS IT MOVES THROUGH THE PIPES IS CALLED WATER PRESSURE.

GO WITH THE FLOW, KIDS.

28

A smaller pipe carried
us to a building.
We went up into
the pipes in the walls.

WATER FACT #9
by Arnold
Water pressure is
usually so strong you
can't keep water from
coming out of an open
faucet with your fingers
no matter how hard
you press.

When a seventh-grader
turned on a faucet
in the girls' bathroom,
we came splashing out.
The building was our school!
We were back!
We were our regular size again!
We were dressed in normal clothes again!
(Except for Ms. Frizzle, of course.)

Back in the classroom,
Ms. Frizzle acted as if
nothing strange had happened.
She started feeding the class lizard.
And she put us to work right away.
We had to make a chart
showing how water gets
to the homes and buildings
in our city.

DOWN, GIRL.

When Arnold drew a picture of
a kid inside a raindrop,
Ms. Frizzle said,
"Where do you *get* these
crazy ideas, Arnold?"

Here is how our water chart turned out.

Later that day,
we saw the old bus
in the school parking lot.
How did *that* get there?
Did we only imagine going through
the water supply system?
Would we ever find out
what *really* happened?

THE LAST TIME
I SAW THAT BUS,
IT WAS IN A CLOUD
. . . I THINK . . .

Ms. Frizzle says we'll be studying
volcanoes next.
This makes us all
feel a little nervous!
After all, with a teacher
like Ms. Frizzle,
*anything* can happen.

THERE AREN'T ANY
VOLCANOS AROUND
HERE, ARE THERE?

VOLCANO

37

# NOTES FROM THE AUTHOR
## (FOR *SERIOUS* STUDENTS ONLY)

The following notes are for serious students who do not like any kidding around when it comes to science facts. If you read these pages, you will be able to tell which facts in this book are true, and which were put in by the author as jokes. (This will also help you decide when to laugh while reading this book.)

On page 8: The green mold that grows on old bread is actually made up of tiny one-celled plants. It *cannot* talk or make any sound whatever.

On page 9: Plants do *not* have hands, *nor* do they wear sunglasses, and the soil does *not* contain burgers, fries, or shakes.

On page 13: Going through a dark tunnel will *not* cause you to wear a scuba diving outfit.

On pages 14-15: The force of gravity keeps a school bus firmly on the ground. It *cannot* rise into the air and enter a cloud, no matter how much you want to miss school that day.

On pages 16-31: Children *cannot* shrink and enter raindrops, fall into streams, or pass through the water purification system. And boys and girls *cannot* come out of the faucet in the girls' bathroom. (Anyone knows boys are not allowed in there.)

On pages 34-35: Your town or city may not get its water from a mountain reservoir, and the purification process may be slightly different from the one in this book. Many towns get water from rivers, lakes, or wells. Do you know where your water comes from and how it is purified?

On page 36: Once a bus is left behind in a cloud, it *cannot* suddenly appear in the school parking lot all by itself. Obviously, someone has to go back to the cloud and drive it home.